Overcoming Perfectionism
How to Let Go of Self-Criticism, Build Self-Esteem, and Find Balance

Clive Reed

Published by Epic Digital

© Copyright 2020 - All rights reserved.

The content contained within this book may not be reproduced, duplicated or transmitted without direct written permission from the author or the publisher.

Under no circumstances will any blame or legal responsibility be held against the publisher, or author, for any damages, reparation, or monetary loss due to the information contained within this book, either directly or indirectly.

Legal Notice:
This book is copyright protected. It is only for personal use. You cannot amend, distribute, sell, use, quote or paraphrase any part, or the content within this book, without the consent of the author or publisher.

Disclaimer Notice:
Please note the information contained within this document is for educational and entertainment purposes only. All effort has been executed to present accurate, up to date, reliable, complete information. No warranties of any kind are declared or implied. Readers acknowledge that the author is not engaged in the rendering of legal, financial, medical or professional advice. The content within this book has been derived from various sources. Please consult a licensed professional before attempting any techniques outlined in this book.

By reading this document, the reader agrees that under no circumstances is the author responsible for any losses, direct or indirect, that are incurred as a result of the use of the information contained within this document, including, but not limited to, errors, omissions, or inaccuracies.

Table of Contents

INTRODUCTION	07
CHAPTER 1: WHAT IS PERFECTIONISM?	09
CHAPTER 2 THE UPSIDES	21
CHAPTER 3: THE DOWNSIDES	34
CHAPTER 4: WHY GOOD IS GOOD ENOUGH	49
CHAPTER 5: PERFECTIONISM IN CHILDREN	63
CHAPTER 6: PERFECTIONISM IN ADULTS	84
CHAPTER 7: STRATEGIES FOR SELF-ACCEPTANCE	99
CHAPTER 8: MINI-LESSONS	120
CONCLUSION	127
REFERENCES	130

Introduction

Do you think you might be a perfectionist? If you're reading this, chances are good that you think you are. Or maybe you're reading this book for someone close to you.

Do you often seek to achieve perfection at work, school and even at home?
Do you feel a need to be perfect at everything you do, even if you know deep down that you might harm your mental and emotional health and well-being?

Of course it is natural to want to be your personal best and avoid pitfalls and mistakes. But mistakes are part of the human experience and cannot be avoided. While perfectionists are often high achievers who relish in the praise they receive for such achievements, they can quickly become emotionally paralyzed, depressed and anxious and lose sight of their goals and potential.

In this book, readers will discover the causes behind perfectionism, learn about the warning signs and impacts of severe problems and discover new strategies for developing the skills necessary to cope with the idea of natural imperfection.

When I began writing this book, I was curious how perfectionism would be technically defined. The definition was not surprising. What struck me was the graph that was included alongside the definition depicting use over time for the word perfection.

A word barely used until the middle of the twentieth century suddenly experienced a dramatic spike in what looks like the 1990s. This makes perfect sense as study after study reports that perfectionistic tendencies have dramatically increased over the past 30 years.

Between 1989 and 2016, one study of American, Canadian, and British college students indicates that the proportion of those students who exhibited traits of perfectionism rose 33 percent.

As we explore perfectionism, its causes and effects and various coping mechanisms, it's important to maintain a focus on questioning this spike.

Chapter 1:
What is Perfectionism?

Perfectionism can turn life into an endless analysis of your daily behavior, accomplishments, appearance and relationships.

At its best, perfectionism can be a motivator and for some people, can provide the drive to overcome adversity, achieve goals and ultimate success.

At its worst, perfectionism can quickly lead down a road of toxic unhappiness, emotional paralysis and emotional instability; thinking that others only value them when they achieve perfection.

Definition

Oxford defines perfectionism as the refusal to accept any standard short of perfection.

When it comes to psychology, people who struggle with perfectionism strive to reach excessively high standards, are overly critical of themselves and are overly concerned about how others judge them.
There is no room for a mistake.

Are You a Perfectionist?

Let's find out. Ask yourself these questions:
- Do you notice errors more than those around you?
- When you see an error, are you the first one to point it out and correct it?
- Do you have a particular way in which you think things should be done?
- Do people describe you as 'all or nothing'?
- Is the end result more important to you than the journey to that end result?
- Are you unusually hard on yourself?
- Is it hard for you to let go of a mistake?
- Do you find yourself wondering 'what if' when things don't go as planned?
- Do you find it hard to feel satisfied?
- Are you likely to wait for the perfect time to begin a task?
- Are you likely to not attempt a task for which a perfect outcome is unlikely?

If you answered yes to the majority of these questions, there is a good chance you have perfectionist tendencies. Perfectionism, like many character traits, live on a sliding scale and although psychologists have built models that categorize perfectionism into different groups, one size does not fit all.

If you dig into research, you will find different types and labels of perfectionism. Here are a few:

Self-oriented perfectionism:
Self-oriented perfectionists have exceptionally high personal standards for themselves. They expect to be perfect and tend to be highly critical of themselves when they inevitably fail to meet these unrealistic high expectations. This kind of person is their own greatest critic.

Socially prescribed perfectionism:
Socially prescribed perfectionists believe that others expect them to be perfect. They believe if they can carry out a task with perfect execution, they will gain acceptance. What's worse is that they believe that their every move is being criticized. Socially prescribed perfectionists tend to be self-deprecating, by poking fun at themselves, often have low self-esteem, find it difficult to deal with stress and feel like they will never measure up.

Other-oriented perfectionism:
This kind of perfectionist is a great critic of others. Other-oriented perfectionists have unreasonably high expectations for others and are highly critical of those who can't or don't meet their expectations. They typically use a caustic and aggressive sense of humor as a way to express disapproval.

Overt perfectionism:
Overt perfectionists like things to be in order and feel anxious without it. They are typically opinionated, like to be right and fear failure to the point where they will often altogether avoid any activity where they are not likely to do well.

Covert perfectionism:
Covert perfectionists have perfectionistic thoughts in their head but hide their perfectionism from the outside world. Covert perfectionists will make it seem like they are flexible and relaxed, but in reality they are internally fixated on succeeding.

Understanding that labels like these exist is important. Identifying that there is a problem with perfectionistic tendencies and expectations is the first step in overcoming them. However, there is no need to put yourself into one of these categories. Many people can see themselves in two or more categories.

The self-destructive beliefs that support perfectionistic tendencies have likely been emotionally hardwired from a young age and can be difficult to acknowledge and even more difficult to overcome.

Dr. Brené Brown writes extensively about vulnerability, shame and perfection. She notes that perfectionists will try to look perfect and be perfect in order to minimize feelings of shame and judgment. We will talk more about Dr. Brown and explore the need to build shame resilience as a critical step to building strategies and skills later in the book.

Steve Jobs Case Study

It's likely that many successful people have struggled with perfectionism but because perfectionism has the stigma of a mental health disorder, we are unlikely to ever really know just how large that number is.

One person who was public about the struggle was Steve Jobs.

For many years, Steve Jobs had tried to persuade biographer Walter Isaacson to write his biography.

When Isaacson realized how sick Jobs was, he finally accepted the task. In an interview with NPR, Isaacson recalls Jobs discussing his perfectionistic tendencies and what he learned from them.

When talking about Jobs' take on perfect, Isaacson recalls:

> I think the ability to connect artistry to science is what made him successful. He was somebody who felt a deep emotional attachment to beauty. He'd sometimes cry when he talked about a beautiful object or when he talked about a letter he was going to write his wife on his anniversary or when he would, you know, talk about an advertising copy for the Think Different ads. He felt poetic beauty was something that made you cry and he drove engineers to be able to do it. To me, that's the real source of his genius.
> He was a tough customer, very demanding.
>
> There's a passion for perfection, and he divides everybody into heroes and dunces. I mean, you know, either you're the best-ever artist, or you totally stink at what you do. And so he could be brutal. But as I said just a moment ago, I try to put it in the context of when he gets the team right, he's able to tell them you can shave 10 seconds off the boot-up time of the Mac. And they say no, that's impossible.

And he convinces them you can do it, and in the end, they shave 28 seconds off of it. So he's able to convince them they can do the impossible, sometimes by being very brusque and rude. He says, look. Brutal honesty is the price of admission for being in the room with me. I can tell you you're full of it. You can tell me I'm full of it. But in the end, they used to give an award at the old Macintosh team of the person who stood up to Steve the best during the year. It was usually won by a woman, you know, Joanna Hofmann, Debbie Coleman. They got promoted. They stuck with Steve.

By the end, he's got - I mean, people would not have stayed with him if he were a true jerk. By the end of his career, both at Apple, everywhere else, he's got a very loyal set of topnotch players who actually are more faithful and loyal and inspired by him than in any other company has. (Flatow, 2011)

Ryan Robinson, an entrepreneur who teaches others how to experience meaningful professional experiences wrote about Steve Jobs. Here is what he said:

> In the early days of Apple, Steve Jobs was well known for his intense perfectionism. Apple spent nearly three years developing the original Macintosh computer, as Jobs demanded final approval of every single detail. This pursuit of what he perceived to be perfection infamously led him to fire talented employees without hesitation for not conforming to his design aesthetics, and to scrap nearly-finished projects that didn't meet his standards for elegance.
>
> While it's certainly true that his attention to detail and relentless drive led the company to create some of the most beautiful (and best) technology products the world has ever seen, his style of leadership was less than admirable in the beginning and had adverse effects on those working at the company.
>
> Eventually, Jobs' demeanor and an internal power struggle over disagreements on philosophies between him and CEO, John Sculley, led to his ousting from the company. In Jobs' eyes, this event was devastating.

Jobs saw his ousting from Apple as an incredible personal failure. He had been pushed out of the company he had worked so hard to grow into a recognizable brand. Before eventually returning to Apple in 1997, Jobs went on to found NeXT and spin Pixar off into its own entity after purchasing the animated division of Lucas Films.

By the time he returned to Apple, Jobs had learned the importance of tempering his obsession with control, and he was much better at empowering his talented employees to do what they do best. Without a doubt, this change in his leadership style is a very significant contributing factor in Apple's return to the spotlight after suffering through some major setbacks during his absence from the company.

Once he returned, he led the charge on Apple's new OS, which redefined how personal computers function, the iPod, which completely revolutionized the music industry, and the iPhone, which has been equally as important in the evolution of personal technological devices.

Although Steve Jobs is no longer with us, he truly changed the world with the products he helped shape, and lessons he imparted along the way. As an entrepreneur, Jobs taught us that it is challenging for a leader to be successful if they're too reckless or unshakable in their way of thinking.

This intense drive for perfection often leads to the failure of young technology companies that should be focusing much more seriously on validating their core product offerings, as opposed to perfecting them straight out the gates. Leaders do need to take risks along the way, pushing for the results they want to see in business while also accepting that there will be failures at times.

In the case of Jobs, he didn't allow his initial failure at Apple to define his life. He went on to learn from his experiences, create more businesses, and eventually return to help make Apple great again. Embracing his failure gave him the motivation to move further forward. (Robsinson, 2019)

Robinson, who feels perfectionism is a form of Obsessive Compulsive Disorder, goes on to say that rather than striving for perfection, he can learn from Jobs' story that balance is really where the magic happens. Balance between done and perfect.

Robinson feels that it's important to remember the positive intentions behind perfection and the positive results that can be achieved. "If you strive to be perfect, which, of course, you never will be, it does mean that you are always attempting to improve on what you are doing. That attitude creates the opportunity for you to come up with truly impressive innovations, as you move toward the state of nirvana you crave—and in theory, since you will be continually improving, you should eventually become an expert in your field" (Haden, n.d.).

Pursuing excellence is not the same as striving for perfection. There are significant benefits of pursuing excellence in all areas of life, but the difference between excellence and perfection lies in the reasonableness of the goal.

For most people, perfection is an unreasonable goal and failure becomes almost certain because you can never achieve the goal.

Points to Remember:

- At its best, perfectionism can be a motivator and for some people, can provide the drive to overcome adversity and achieve goals and ultimate success.

- At its worst, perfectionism can quickly lead down a road of toxic unhappiness, emotional paralysis and emotional instability, thinking that others only value them when they achieve perfection.

- There are several types of perfectionism. Identifying the type or types that most closely apply to your situation can help in getting started on the path to coping and happiness.

Chapter 2
The Upsides

When one person labels another as a perfectionist, it is often meant as a compliment. And it's often taken that way too.

Our culture tends to view perfectionists in a positive light. Those seeking self-improvement need only look to a quick search online or - gasp - at the bookstore to find loads of resources about how to be more productive and efficient, how to do, manage and earn more on less sleep. Every television channel you turn to has the perfect house being built or the perfect meal being laid out on the table. Then you see your friends posting only the perfect versions of their life on social media.

Perfectionists are perceived to be passionate about giving their best and achieving their best in every area of their lives. They are meticulous about crossing their t's and dotting their i's. Every day. In everything they do.

In their professional lives, those perceived as perfectionists put extra hours into preparing for presentations. Editing their work and editing it again. Rehearsing, anticipating the things that may go wrong and planning for contingencies.

You know that feeling. There really is no report, no email, no presentation that wouldn't benefit from one more round of tweaks and edits.

Perfectionists put a lot of value on success. Doesn't sound so bad. Success is a good thing, isn't it?

Perfectionists can use their tendencies to achieve precise standards that exceed the expectations of many.

The problem occurs when the expectations of the perfectionist are never met. No matter how much work went into a project, it's just never quite good enough. It is impossible to excel in every area. It is unrealistic, self-defeating and self-destructive to expect otherwise.

While many would argue that there is no upside to being a perfectionist, it's worth exploring a few ideas.

Positive Perfectionists?

Is there a difference between striving for excellence and being a perfectionist?

Researchers have suggested that forms of perfectionism that involve high personal standards can be positive and label them as adaptive. These studies cite world-class athletes as an example. The athletes have unusually high standards, but are not, and shouldn't be, labeled as pathological or perfectionist just because they shoot for the stars.

Possessing some perfectionistic tendencies can be healthy if they motivate you toward a better work ethic and a more concerted effort in the face of a challenge. Pouring your heart and soul into a goal and accomplishing something that pushes you beyond your comfort zone is positive, rewarding and overall a very good thing. In order to avoid the downsides and steer clear of perfectionism, it is critical to acknowledge the importance of the effort itself rather than only the outcome.

Adaptive perfectionists, sometimes referred to as positive perfectionists, are thought by some to be those who strive for excellence whereas maladaptive perfectionists, sometimes called negative perfectionists, are failure oriented.

Positive perfectionists are those who set high standards and are relentless in their pursuit of success. Their tendencies are seen as strengths rather than weaknesses.

The silver linings to a rather stringent personality trait are seen as:
- hard work
- achievement-oriented nature
- dependability
- problem solvers at heart
- desire for growth
- enjoyment of challenge
- some health benefits

This is a controversial issue.
Dr. Paul Hewitt, PhD, has no patience for researchers who argue that perfectionism can sometimes serve as a healthy motivation for reaching ambitious goals.
For more than 20 years, Hewitt has researched perfectionism and how it correlates with depression, anxiety, eating disorders and other mental health problems.

While high standards are part of perfectionist tendencies, having high standards doesn't necessarily make one a perfectionist.

Those people who have high standards and don't fall apart when those standards aren't met will fare much better than their maladaptive counterparts who have equally high standards but simply can't handle when those standards are not met.

Type A Personality or Perfectionism?

If you fear that you might be a perfectionist, then you have very likely been referred to as 'type A'. That label probably doesn't sting as sharply.

After all, what is wrong with being ambitious, driven and organized? Those are admirable traits that lead to successful lives.

You can't live without a to-do-list. Or two. Or three. So what?

When these positive aspects of the personality traits are much greater than the negative aspects—like impatience, frustration, self-loathing and competitiveness—then you might very likely see the upsides of being labeled type A.

Many don't realize that type A isn't even a real thing. It's not an actual clinical term. Rather, it is a social label that became popular in the '70s to describe a cluster of perfectionist personality traits. But just because it isn't a clinical term, does that mean it can be more easily managed?

The answer is maybe. There are certainly things you can do to accentuate the positive and diminish the negative impacts. Although we will explore strategies later in the book, below are a few ways to check yourself and keep your type A tendencies from becoming a clinical problem, assuming they aren't already there.

Advice for Emphasizing the Positive

Know Thyself

Identifying perfectionist thought patterns is often the first step. In which areas of your life do you most often exhibit these traits?

Let's take your home life. Wanting to keep a tidy house is not a bad thing. The positives here are many. A clean and clutter-free home can keep other perfectionist tendencies from manifesting. However, being aware of any negative aspects that result from the need to keep your home a certain way is essential. For example, does keeping the home clean get in the way of your personal relationship with your spouse or children? Are you able to relax when entertaining and not focus on the mess that inevitably results during an event?

Reflect upon each area and ask yourself some serious questions. When you spot behavior that seems like it rests on a slippery slope, pay attention and be honest with yourself. Is this just being ambitious, driven and organized, or is it a bigger problem?

Reflect on Your Communication Style

If you are keeping your perfectionist tendencies in check, you are able to hold yourself to slightly higher, although reasonable, standards than those around you while also interacting with them in a calm, warm, considerate and patient manner the majority of the time.

Red flags arise when you're so tightly wound that your feelings or impatience or frustration consistently manifest in your communication with others.

Of course, no one is perfect and calm all of the time, but if you find that you are not projecting in the way you'd like, there might be a bigger problem.

It's Not All About You

Think about how you interpret and perceive different situations and interactions.

When a co-worker behaves in a less than courteous way on a Monday morning do you attribute it to a long weekend or do you take it as a personal affront to something you did wrong or your personal identity as a whole?

Give some thought to your thought patterns. Realize that it is often not about you at all.

If this is an issue for you, developing a strategy—like counting to five with a few deep breaths to remind yourself it's probably them and probably not you—can be effective.

Think in Terms of North Star

Those who have unhealthy perfectionist tendencies treat ideals like goals, which must be achieved otherwise the work to get there is purposeless.

Those who have only the healthy pieces of perfectionist tendencies treat ideals like a North Star and appreciate the steps it takes in moving toward it.

Although cliché, life really is not about the destination but about the journey.

See the Big Picture

No matter in which category you are beginning to see yourself, it is critical to remember that you are more than just your perfectionist traits. Stop labeling yourself and realize that you are made up of many traits and qualities, just like everyone else. Good traits and bad.

No matter where you fall on the spectrum of perfectionism, that is only part of your story.

Views on Defeat

How do you react to failure?

For high achievers, even those without any perfectionist personality traits, this one can be challenging to say the least. To perform effectively in any aspect of life, accepting failure and moving forward is a must. In today's environment, things move at lightning speed. There is no time to lament mistakes. If you can't get up and dust yourself off, ready to try again, you'll be left behind.

The Race

Hopefully, you are beginning to see that distinguishing between positive perfection and negative perfection is not black and white.

Perfection is one of those things that one day feels like something to be proud of and the next it brings about feelings of shame. Society rewards us for being the best and constantly raising the bar.

Research even shows that students who wanted to be perceived in a more positive light by peers and professors describe themselves as perfectionists.
Positive and negative perfectionists set high standards for themselves. They both work hard.

Sometimes the line between positive and negative is almost invisible. The difference is that positive perfectionists are achievement oriented and negative perfectionists are failure oriented.

As we explore an area with so much gray, this metaphor about a race might help.

Winning the race is important to both positive and negative perfectionists. It is the reason for wanting to win that is the differentiator.

Positive perfectionists have the natural desire to win for the sake of winning. They want their hard work to pay off. It's pretty simple. All throughout their training, they are driven to win largely by the desire for growth. If they lose, they will not crumble or give up because the main focus was on the satisfaction gained from training and improving. The loss provides an opportunity for self-reflection and improvement, not for self-loathing.

Negative perfectionists, on the other hand, focus on not losing. It's not about what they want, it's more about what they don't want. They don't want to lose. They don't want to be embarrassed. They don't want the other team to win. Losing for them will have a very different outcome than for the positive perfectionist. When negative perfectionistic personality traits dominate, it is time to consider getting help. We will explore the downsides, some which are cause for extreme concern, in the next chapter.

Points to Remember:

- Our culture tends to view perfectionists in a positive light.
- The problem occurs when the expectations of the perfectionist are never met.
- While many would argue that there is no upside to being a perfectionist, it's worth exploring a few ideas.
- Possessing some perfectionistic tendencies can be healthy if they motivate you toward a better work ethic and a more concerted effort in the face of a challenge.
- While high standards are part of perfectionist tendencies, having high standards doesn't necessarily make one a perfectionist.
- Identifying perfectionist thought patterns is often the first step.
- Red flags arise when you're so tightly wound that your feelings or impatience or frustration consistently manifest in your communication with others.
- Think about how you interpret and perceive different situations and interactions. Realize that it is often not about you at all.
- Those who have only the healthy pieces of perfection tendencies treat ideals like a North

Star and appreciate the steps it takes in moving toward it.
- Stop labeling yourself and realize that you are made up of many traits and qualities, just like everyone else. Good traits and bad.
- To perform effectively in any aspect of life, accepting failure and moving forward is a must.
- Distinguishing between positive perfection and negative perfection is not black and white.

Chapter 3:
The Downsides

Perfectionists are viewed as high achievers who strive to be the best athletes, ace exams, quickly climb the corporate ladder and raise those perfect children you see in advertisements for yacht attire.

Given these social perceptions, it can be easy to mistake this drive for perfection as perfection itself and assume these people are the picture of physical, emotional and mental health.

Obviously this is not the case and study after study proves that perfection can cause many problems. In some ways, perfection can be a positive virtue, but beyond a certain point has the potential to backfire and become a very dangerous impediment.

In order to determine whether you are operating as a positive or negative perfectionist, understanding the downsides of being a perfectionist must be explored.

Impact on Mental and Emotional Health

While positive perfectionists have been shown to be healthier psychologically, more emotionally stable, and better protected from emotional distress, studies have shown that those with negative perfectionism are likely to use emotional suppression as a coping mechanism and demonstrate increased tendencies for depression, regret and even cognitive dysfunction.

Negative perfectionism has been linked to increased anxiety, decreased self-esteem and increased rates of depression.

Impact on Suicidal Tendencies

According to an AIPC suicide follow back study, over half of people who died as a result of suicide were described by loved ones as perfectionists.

One study showed that perfectionism had associations with increased suicidal thoughts.
Perfectionists concerned with the perceived expectations of others were more associated with suicide attempts than those perfectionists who hold others to high standards. Perfectionists who were concerned with tidiness and organization were not related to suicidal thoughts or attempts.

"Perfectionists," the researchers explained, "are their own worst critics … locked in an endless loop of self-defeating over-striving in which each new task is another opportunity for harsh self-rebuke, disappointment, and failure" (Jarrett, 2017, para 7).

The most dangerous form of perfectionism continues to be around meeting the expectations of others.

This type was related to increased suicidal thoughts in continuing studies that followed the same participants over time. "Our findings lend credence to the long-standing notion that feeling incapable of living up to the lofty standards of others is a part of the premorbid personality of people at risk for suicide," the researchers said (Jarrett, 2017, para 8).

Research around this topic is lacking as of the date this book was written. Most research to date has only involved white Western individuals. For now, however, the research is certainly disturbing and seems to prove that perfectionism is in fact associated with intense psychological pain and that perfectionists have a "harsh way of relating to a self they find deficient" (Jarrett, 2017, para 11).

Impact on Physical Health

Many studies have been conducted regarding perfectionism's impact on mental health, but relatively few have looked at the toll on physical health. Various ailments like migraines, chronic pain and asthma have been linked with perfectionism.

According to Professor Gordon Flett who studies perfectionism extensively, "Recent studies continue to suggest that the costs of perfectionism outweigh the benefits." He goes on to say, "Some of the largest costs associated with perfectionism may be in terms of poor health" (Flett, 2012, paras 2-3). He is not surprised since unrelenting perfectionism can easily result in chronic stress.

High blood pressure seems to be more prevalent among perfectionistic people, and has even been linked to cardiovascular disease. In addition, perfectionists will have a harder time coping with physical ailments. Among the ailments studied were Chrohn's disease, ulcerative colitis and heart attack.

When we experience stress, physiological changes take place in the body. The adrenal glands release neurotransmitters to prepare the body for fight-or-flight syndrome. This results in increased heart rate, metabolic rate and blood pressure and dilated airways and coronary arteries.

When fight or flight kicks in, blood flow to areas of the body not needed for that fight or flight, like your immune and digestive systems, is reduced. Imagine hitting the pause button on them.

In most people, fight or flight is temporary and the ancillary systems—like the immune system—can resume play and 'unpause' if you will. But for perfectionists, the stress response is prolonged and the body feels as if it is always in a state of danger, which means that the immune system will ultimately suffer.

A study in 2011 at Tehran University in Iran studied the physiology of perfectionists in stressful situations. When compared to people who were more controlled and resilient, the perfectionists experienced significantly more stress.

Perfectionists are also more likely to be insomniacs. A study by the University of Coimbra in Portugal found that perfectionists had more difficulty falling asleep and staying asleep than other students.

Impact on Lifespan

Prem Fry, a psychology professor at Trinity Western University in Canada, studied the relationship between perfectionism and overall risk of death in 450 adults aged 65 and older for 6.5 years in 2010. An initial questionnaire assessed levels of perfectionism and other personality traits.

Participants with high perfectionism scores, had a 51% increased risk of death compared to those with low perfectionism scores. Fry's team attributes high levels of stress and anxiety might have contributed to the decreased lifespan.

However, it should be noted that when Fry's team studied those with chronic disease, they found surprising results. The team assumed that the increased stress related with perfectionism would be detrimental. However, the opposite was true. Those with high perfectionism scores had a 26% lower risk of death than those with low perfectionism scores.

These results suggest that in certain situations, perfectionism can have advantages. With type 2 diabetes, for example, meticulous monitoring of blood sugar levels and strict adherence to dietary rules can pay dividends by reducing the severity of the disease.

"In this particular study on diabetes, those kinds of perfectionistic attitudes, normally we would regard them to be dysfunctional attitudes, but in the case of the diabetic sample, they turned out to be very positive traits," Fry said. "These individuals were highly self-critical, they worked harder than the average person to adhere to the instructions of the physician or the attending doctor in staying with all the do's and don'ts of diabetic diet constraints" (Rettner, 2010, para 23).

These positive results should be considered in conjunction with data that shows that the same high standards that enabled these individuals with diabetes to reduce the severity of their disease can also translate to added pressure on oneself when mistakes in self-care are made. This can lead to increased resistance against asking for help for fear of revealing weakness and imperfection.

Overall, perfectionism is linked to weaker overall physical health and an increased risk of death.

Naturally, different personality types and the different types of perfectionism can contribute to the results. Some perfectionists with solid social networks tend to be happier just as the general population also thrives with social connection.

However, depending on the situation and your particular predisposition to perfectionism, you may also receive a significant amount of support from your social network, but interpret it in the incorrect way. Even when others reach out to help, many perfectionists interpret that help as critical or an acknowledgment of imperfection, which can lead to a downward spiral of depression.

However, perfectionists with isolating tendencies generally remove themselves over time from various elements of their lives, and when this happens health diminishes.

Another contributing factor in diminished health is the tendency for perfectionists to provide themselves with very little, if any, self-care.

Impact on Professional Performance

Diligent workers are very different from perfectionists. Diligent workers pay attention to details, are meticulously on time and prompt with deadlines and tend to climb the corporate ladder relatively faster than those with a less rigorous work ethic.

However, perfectionists operate differently, especially negative perfectionists. At work, perfectionists tend to operate in their own silo. You may have heard this referred to as working like a "lone ranger".

Negative perfectionists have such extreme expectations for themselves and for others that it can lead to:

- cognitive rigidity
- difficulty when collaborating with others as part of a team
- excessive concentration on minute details
- procrastination
- decision atrophy
- career stagnation

Perfectionists can often keep working on a project even when the level of effort is far outweighing the benefit of those efforts. They have a hard time stopping the editing and revising process. They can't seem to put the pencil down. In essence, their investment in the project will far outweigh the returns.

This leads to burnout and frustration. By trying to achieve perfection at work, perfectionists often miss out on the big picture.

What about the team work?
What about the learning process?
Nobody wants to be around a coworker who is constantly burned out and frustrated. While the perfectionist is trying to achieve an unrealistic goal, the rest of the team is likely to have been either left out of the process or treated poorly along the way.

Because failure is a critical part of the learning process, the constant struggle to avoid mistakes at all costs will hold a perfectionist back from reaching even higher goals. The same is true for those with whom they work.

In the workplace, perfectionism holds those who struggle with it back from performing effectively and productively. With their minds in constant conflict, and focused on perfection rather than simply completing a specific task well, it can be impossible to play the long game and achieve real professional success.

Again, the extent of the professional problems one perfectionist will experience will be different than another's. One person might simply have a persistent feeling of dissatisfaction, while another might be significantly crippled and eventually end up not being able to do their job. It's a slippery slope.

Negative Self-Talk

Perfectionists are not easy to please. While working on a project, it is very likely that a perfectionist would see the first version of the deliverable and not be satisfied.

However, positive perfectionists and negative perfectionists will talk to themselves silently inside the mind in very different ways.

Positive perfectionists are more likely to think, "It can be better" and focus on the future product being improved. Hard work ensues quickly after acknowledging the mistakes or oversights in order to get a promotion or simply for the satisfaction of a job well done.

Negative perfectionists take a more punitive tone in their minds and would be more likely to think, "It's not good enough." Hard work ensues slowly after spending a good deal of time and energy shaking one's head and lots of negative self-talk. The hard work has the ultimate goal of avoiding a bad review, avoiding being fired, or preventing a promotion from going to a coworker.

Being hard on yourself takes a toll. If whenever something goes wrong, you give yourself a tongue-lashing, self-esteem is going to take a major hit and the cycle continues to spiral out of control.

Procrastination

Negative perfectionists tend to develop unrealistic visions for how things should be. As a result, working on any sort of task or project can become challenging. Because they tend to obsess about even the smallest details being perfect, and this is often impossible, perfectionists can tend to put off the work involved with a task because perfection can't be achieved.

It might not be the right time.
They might not have the right equipment.
The results may seem unlikely to be achieved.

Missing the Journey

For perfectionists, everything is about the end result. They aren't concerned with the journey to get there or the learning processes along the way as long as the end result is perfect. When this doesn't happen, feelings of annoyance and even devastation can result.

Because of the unreasonably high standards, the stress can be overwhelming. At some point, perfectionists become crippled by these standards and stop working on their goals altogether simply out of fear that perfection can't be achieved.

Perfectionists often have very low latent inhibition, which means they are extremely sensitive to surrounding stimuli. They notice sounds, visuals, words, feelings, and behaviors more than others.

This leads to seeing more mistakes than other people see. Sometimes these mistakes are real, but sometimes they are imagined. What you focus on becomes bigger in your mind. So, perfectionists often end up focusing on the negative and missing the positive elements of life's journey.

It is Possible to Turn it All Around

According to Ann Smith, negative perfectionism can be mitigated. We are all unique and flawed. It's part of the experience as human beings. Don't judge your flaws or the flaws of others. Embrace mistakes and missteps and see them as part of being human.

Amazing things happen when you let go - even a little.

Here are some tips that will be explored further throughout the book.
1. Put other people first. Instead of focusing on making yourself perfect, put that effort into connecting with those around you.

2. Accept being human. Embrace it. Being authentic enables us to live life with joy and self-love. It might be messy and sometimes embarrassing, but it's real.
3. Take it one step at a time. Rather than trying to completely shut down negative self-talk, for example, just try to minimize it. Rather than trying to stop comparing yourself to others entirely, aim to recognize when it is happening so you can then move to the next stop of reducing that behavior.
4. Remember that kids learn when they make mistakes. Looking and acting perfect is much less important than being happy.

Reward yourself for the small efforts along the way and remember that it is never too late to push back against perfectionistic tendencies.

Points to Remember:

- In some ways, perfection can be a positive virtue, but beyond a certain point has the potential to backfire and become a very dangerous impediment.

- In order to determine whether you are operating as a positive or negative perfectionist, understanding the downsides of being a perfectionist must be explored.
- Those with negative perfectionism are likely to use emotional suppression as a coping mechanism and demonstrate increased tendencies for depression, regret, and even cognitive dysfunction.
- The most dangerous form of perfectionism continues to be around meeting the expectations of others.
- Various ailments like migraines, chronic pain and asthma have been linked with perfectionism.
- Diminished health often results as perfectionists tend to provide themselves with very little, if any, self-care.
- Being hard on yourself takes a toll.
- Perfectionists often end up focusing on the negative and missing the positive elements of life's journey.

Chapter 4:
Why Good is Good Enough

The consequences of perfectionism have been well studied. Even the causes of perfectionism have received some attention through examining how a familiar environment contributes to the character trait. However, not much research has been focused upon society's impact and the evolution of perfectionism.

There was a time when good was good enough. In order to understand when this began to change in our society, we can look at a study performed in 2019 focused on cultural changes that contribute to the rise in perfectionistic tendencies. The study cites three major contributing factors (Curran, 2019):

Competitive Individualism

Cultural values have significantly changed in recent decades. Since the late 1970s, several events have triggered social and economic transformation. These changes have given rise to increased competition that have led to changes in how young people develop their identities.

For example, college students in the United States today report higher levels of narcissism, extraversion, and self-confidence than previous generations and lower levels of concern for communal causes. Recent generations of college students show less empathy toward others and are more likely to blame victims when things go wrong.

The study found that young people spend less time doing group activities for fun and more time doing individual activities that produce results for themselves or a sense of personal achievement.

Behaviors associated with competition and social standing have risen. Across the world, people are becoming increasingly preoccupied with upward social comparison. They unsurprisingly experience increasing levels of status anxiety as a result and end up becoming materialistic in an effort to perfect their lives as they compare those lives to those of others.

Even in a time in history where more people recognize Kim Kardashian than they do the Speaker of the House of Representatives, the following statistics might be shocking:
- For 81% of Americans born in the 1980s, becoming materially rich is among their most important life goals. This is almost 20% higher than those born in the 1960s and 1970s.
- Younger generations borrow more heavily than did older generations at the same point

- in their lives and spend, on average, a much greater proportion of their income on material possessions that signify state than their parents.
- Young people are more dissatisfied with what they have and also seemingly more dissatisfied with who they are.

Social media naturally plays a part in all of this. Facebook, Instagram, and Snapchat have become part of the daily routine and are reported to occupy at least two out of every five minutes spent online.

Social media allows users to curate a perfect public image. However, seeing the perfect public images of other people tends to exacerbate feelings of anxiety, social isolation and alienation and a host of others.

Social malaise has been on the rise, but now cultural values are shifting toward individualism more and more every day. Language patterns, the media, materialistic behavior and social media are shaping the identities of children and adults alike and pushing the concept of the perfectible self.

All of this leads to "fear of negative social evaluation, characterized by a focus on deficiencies, and sensitive to criticism and failure" (Curran, 2019, p.413).

Sound familiar?

The shift toward competitive individualism results in the adoption of the ideas that:
- humans are perfectible
- perfection is desirable and attainable
- achieving perfection will provide safety, connection and self-worth

Meritocracy

You have likely noticed the spike in college tuition over the past few decades. College campuses, once old brick buildings focused solely on the learning happening inside, have morphed into state-of-the-art sprawling corporate-like complexes.

Meritocracy has something to do with this.
Meritocracy is the idea that the achievement, wealth and, of course, social status associated with a perfect life are available to anyone who tries hard enough. Those who try hard deserve entry to top schools. They deserve occupations that pay the highest salaries.

Meritocracy is the belief that those who don't reach these heights are somehow less deserving. They didn't try hard enough or they just don't have the ability. In essence, meritocracy links professional achievement with innate personal value and therefore places the need to perform and achieve at the center of today's meaning of life.

One place meritocracy has had the most significant impact has been in education. Historically, the purpose of education was to provide young people with a broad array of skills and knowledge. It was more about the journey. Today, the purpose of education is tightly linked to economic success and potential market value.

By merging academic and economic goals, expectations begin to become unrealistic.

Parental Practices

You knew this one was coming. We've all heard the term helicopter parent. You've seen parents fighting at youth athletic events. Parents have seemingly lost control of themselves in trying to control the lives of their children.

This study found that parents not only feel responsible for their own success, but in today's world feel increasingly responsible for the success and failure of their children. There is actually a term for this: child-contingent self-esteem.

Child-contingent self-esteem has caused parental expectations for their kids' achievements to reach never before seen levels. Increases in anxious and controlling behavior in parents help explain why perfectionism is on the rise. The study reports that parents are:

- spending far more time with their children on academic activities and less time on leisure activities or hobbies
- since the early 1990s, mothers in the United States have reallocated over 9 hours per week from leisure time to childcare, including 2 additional hours per week afforded specifically to education
- feeling increased pressure to secure a successful future for their children and that pressure has had significant effects on the parenting experience
- resorting to more anxious and overly controlling parental styles as a result of passing their own achievement anxieties onto their children
- monitoring children's whereabouts and activities more
- less likely to show interest in children's ideas

How Can We Find Our Way Back

The "Good Enough" Mother

When many hear the phrase "good enough" they hear "not enough". Let's face it, in our society, at some point being good enough became not enough.

While perfectionism has been on the rise since the 1970s, this concept of "good enough" was being studied long before. Two decades before, in fact.

In 1953, the phrase "good enough mother" was coined by a British pediatrician and psychoanalyst named David Winnicott. As he observed thousands of mothers and babies, he discovered that babies and children benefit from normal parenting fails. By normal he meant not providing them with complete attentiveness at all times, not child abuse or neglect.

A child actually needs the parent to "fail" them on a regular basis in order for the child to learn to live in our very imperfect world.

Every time parents don't run when their children call, every time parents feed them a meal they don't want to eat, every time parents don't buy the new item that kids think would make their life as perfect as everyone else's, they prepare their kids for a society that is often frustrating and disappointing on a regular basis. Essentially, Winnicott found that by being only "good enough" parents can build resilience in their children.

Winnicott didn't coin the term because he was ok settling for second-best, but because he saw the toll perfectionism was taking on parents. He knew that in order to live a happy life, parents had to learn not to hate themselves for failing to be what no human being can ever be—perfect.

This concept doesn't relate only to parenting, but to every aspect of life.

A relationship can be good enough despite the everyday problems and even despite more serious problems.

A job can be good enough even though it has its boring days and you're not a billionaire. If you're establishing fulfilling relationships and sometimes experience motivation, excitement and accomplishment, you're probably doing alright.
It's all about how we see our experience.

Winnicott's concept of good enough is all about the bravery it takes to live a good life, even an ordinary one. To keep your chin up and quietly persevere through the everyday challenges we all experience in relationships, parenting and work is quite a heroic achievement.

Good Enough in Today's World

Deconstruct what it means to accept good enough instead of perfection. It doesn't mean accepting second best. It doesn't mean settling for less. Rather, it means doing your best and knowing that is enough.

We will delve into strategies in a later chapter, but below are several ways to begin adopting a "good enough" mindset.

Forget the Joneses. Put your blinders on. Worry about your three-foot world. Whatever it takes to ignore what others are doing or achieving. In a culture fixated on social media, this can be hard to do.

First you must spend some time understanding and thinking about the fact that comparison only validates our self-doubts. It never leaves you feeling better about yourself. Even if you see that your life is somehow exceeding that of another, deep down you know that reveling in that fact is wrong.

Then you must also understand that what you are seeing on social media is the shiny touched up version of someone else's life. In fact even in a face-to-face interaction, this is often what you are also seeing. So comparing the real you to the shiny version of others is simply not a fair comparison.

Learn about growth mindset. Becoming aware of how the brain operates and its power over your thinking patterns can provide relief in knowing that your best effort is good enough. Those with a growth mindset believe that skills can be developed and understand that hard work in itself is success.

Adopting a growth mindset can also help you stop trying to keep up with Joneses. Growth mindset places emphasis on comparing yourself against yourself. You end up looking at who you were last year and who you are today. Now, that's a fair comparison.

More about growth mindset in Chapter 5.

Learn when to stop. Reworking a report 16 times is not necessary. Somewhere after the second revision, you aren't even moving the needle. In fact, reworking so relentlessly can actually diminish the quality of your work.

Set a timer for yourself when working on a project. Limits, even if they are self-imposed and artificial, can help in avoiding procrastination and nurture acceptance of good enough.

Writer, comedian and actor Tina Fey discusses how good enough is an important concept in her own work:

> [At *Saturday Night Live*] the show doesn't go on because it's ready; it goes on because it's eleven-thirty...it's a great lesson in not being too precious about your writing. You have to try your hardest to be at the top of your game and improve every joke until the last possible second, but then you have to let it go.
>
> You can't be that kid standing at the top of the waterslide, overthinking it. You have to go down the chute. (And I'm from a generation in which a lot of people died on waterslides, so this was an important lesson for me to learn.) You have to let people see what you wrote. It will never be perfect, but perfect is overrated. Perfect is boring on live television.

What I learned about bombing as an improviser at Second City was that, while bombing is painful, it doesn't kill you. What I learned about bombing as a writer for "Saturday Night Live" is that you can't be too worried about your permanent record. Yes, you're going to write some sketches that you love and are proud of forever—your golden nuggets. But you're also going to write some real shit nuggets. You can't worry about it. As long as you know the difference, you can go back to panning for gold on Monday." (Fey, 2011, paras 14-16)

Replace perfection with persistence. Start by recognizing what is realistic and what is not. Strive for persistence, perseverance, resilience, and flexibility. Traits like these will produce better work than perfectionism will. And you'll be much happier at the end of the day.

With perfection, you're fighting a losing battle. If you guide your work with these new traits, even if things go wrong, you can rest your head on the pillow at night knowing you gave it your best and that was good enough.

Points to Remember:

- Cultural values have significantly changed in recent decades.
- Behaviors associated with competition and social standing have risen.
- Studies have found that young people spend less time doing group activities for fun and more time doing individual activities that produce results for themselves or a sense of personal achievement.
- Social media allows users to curate a perfect public image. However, seeing the perfect public images of other people tends to exacerbate feelings of anxiety, social isolation and alienation and a host of others.
- Studies have found that parents not only feel responsible for their own success, but in today's world feel increasingly responsible for the success and failure of their children.
- A child actually needs the parent to "fail" them on a regular basis in order for the child to learn to live in our very imperfect world.
- The concept of *good enough* is all about the bravery it takes to live a good life - even an ordinary one. To keep your chin up and quietly persevere through the everyday challenges we all experience in relationships,

parenting and work is quite a heroic achievement.
- Becoming aware of how the brain operates and its power over your thinking patterns can provide relief in knowing that your best effort is good enough.
- Limits, even if they are self-imposed and artificial, can help in avoiding procrastination and nurturing acceptance of good enough.
- Strive for persistence, perseverance, resilience, and flexibility. Traits like these will produce better work than perfectionism will.

Chapter 5:
Perfectionism in Children

Shocking data and facts can be found about perfectionism in children. It's probably no surprise that young people struggle with body image in our very visual culture that promotes unrealistic body ideals. You probably already knew that, since the advent of social media, eating disorders and related body dysmorphia issues have been on the rise.

However, it might shock you to know that today's young people are increasingly choosing to have plastic surgery in an effort to achieve physical perfection.

Is social media to blame? Are parents to blame? Or are certain people predisposed to perfectionism? Let's take a look.

What Causes Perfectionism?

Nature vs. Nurture

Although many think overbearing parents are to blame, an increasing number of studies suggests that the parents' perfectionist genes may actually bear a larger portion of the blame.

In one study, researchers examined perfectionism in "146 pairs of identical and fraternal female twins ages 12 to 22. Identical twins—which share 100% of their genetic makeup—scored similarly on tests measuring perfectionism and anxiety. Meanwhile, fraternal twins—which share only 50% of their genetic makeup—recorded less similar scores on measures of perfectionism and anxiety" (Advisory Board, 2012, para 2).

Parental Influence

In many families, perfectionism is encouraged, knowingly or unknowingly. Young children have a strong desire to please their parents and are therefore at the mercy of their parents during a critical time in their lives. They are building self-worth, resilience and their own ideas about success and failure.

Children don't have the cognitive ability to differentiate between normal expectations and abusive expectations. They simply don't yet understand that adults are often wrong. If a parent consistently communicates a negative message to a child, the child is very likely to believe the parent and internalize this as a self-image.

The child will find evidence that supports the image and make connections that further internalize the negative self-image. Tell a child she's too fat, she'll find a way to believe you. Tell a child he's not smart enough, he'll find evidence to prove you're right.

Parents who levy harsh punishments on children for mistakes are also encouraging perfectionism. Parents are delivering the message that mistakes will not be tolerated. The degree of abusiveness can vary and might include name-calling, yelling, the silent treatment, and even physical punishment.

It may not be this sinister, however. Children can also learn perfectionism just by growing up around highly successful parents, perfectionists or not, who model perfection through expectations for themselves and their behavior.

Perfectionism can also be encouraged when parents praise children excessively for achievements rather than for their efforts or progress. Children who receive praise only for the A rather than all the hard work that went into it are more likely to develop perfectionistic tendencies. Children can begin to see perfection as the only way to gain a parent's love and acceptance.

Coping Mechanism

Family life can be to blame even if parents do not expect perfection. Children can impose perfection on themselves.

Some children develop perfectionistic tendencies as a coping mechanism for an unpredictable, chaotic or even abusive homelife. Children feel the need to have control over some element of their lives, so they resort to restricting their diet or achieving perfection at school.

Societal Influence

Society, the media, and especially social media have significant influence on perfectionism. Most images that young people see feature models who are tall and impossibly thin. When children grow up bombarded with these unattainable images, they begin to see themselves in comparison.

Social Media

Children are growing up with increased access to social media that encourages comparison. Not only through the information and images being posted, but through the number of likes those posts receive.

Social media also triggers the fear of missing out, commonly known as FOMO. Children don't have the perspective to realize that what is posted on social media is only part of the story. They don't understand that the shiny versions being shared have another side complete with problems, tough times and insecurities.

You don't need statistics to prove how prevalent social media is in today's society. Researchers of perfectionism knew that social media would have massive impacts and would also provide massive opportunities to further study the character trait. Before social media, only celebrities had access to such platforms. Now anyone with basic tech skills can be a mass communicator.

Perfectionists by nature will try to control how they are perceived in everyday face-to-face interactions. However, in real life there is always the chance of a mistake or a slip-up. Never before have they had such high levels of control over how precisely they present themselves.

With this increased control of how a person presents themselves, perfectionists are especially likely to struggle with which self to present—the real self or the ideal self. Perfectionists spend time and effort editing, deleting and creating their ideal self to remove any less than perfect images. This can easily become a problem.

Research examined the relationship between the level of Facebook use and the mental well-being of college students in 2011. The number of Facebook friends had an inverse relationship on mental health, meaning that students with more Facebook friends performed poorer academically and socially, which caused a greater degree of negative effects on mental well-being.

Case Study: The Like Button
Justin Rosenstein worked at Facebook in 2007. He was part of a small group who brainstormed how Facebook could allow people to send each other positive reactions to posted material. Rosenstein pulled several all-nighters to design a prototype of what was originally called the 'awesome button'. The 'like' was born. Rosenstein says the feature was "wildly successful: engagement soared as people enjoyed the short-term boost they got from giving or receiving social affirmation, while Facebook harvested valuable data about the preferences of users that could be sold to advertisers" (Lewis, 2017, para 10).

Soon after Twitter and Instagram followed and the rest is history.

But now Rosenstein is attempting to disassociate himself from all of that hard work, saying, "It is very common for humans to develop things with the best of intentions and for them to have unintended, negative consequences" (Lewis, 2017, para 5).

The unintended consequences are more than just negative—they can be downright debilitating. Not only has the like button deepened the political divide, but in young people and adults alike, likes encourage comparison. Young people are fixated on the number of likes a post is receiving. And they aren't just fixated on their own posts and those likes, but they monitor their friends' posts and their former friends' posts to see how many likes those posts receive. Song lyrics even refer to likes and offer advice for how to identify a girl with low self-esteem: look for posts with very few likes.

Social media has also been proven to negatively impact the mental health of young people, especially teenagers. At such a critical time for development of identity and understanding social norms, social media can confuse young people. They are not sure whether they are experiencing real or only perceived support through the platform.

Importance on social capital becomes distorted. How they measure their self-worth becomes tied up in elements of society they don't even understand yet.

Comments, likes and posts contribute to feelings of self-worth and the lack of those things can contribute to feelings of worthlessness, anxiety, body-image disorders and more. Perfectionists will have a particularly difficult time with all of these consequences.

Some social media platforms have taken notice. Instagram announced that it will roll out a platform without likes. The intention behind this move has been debated. Facebook, which owns Instagram, maintains that it will hide likes in an effort to reduce bullying and mental health issues of users. They want to depressurize the platform and make it less competitive.

However, some hypothesize that the company realizes the degree of power behind the like and the fact that more people would be inclined to use Instagram if likes weren't public. So essentially the move is motivated by the company's desire to drive usage. Either way, hiding likes could be a step in the right direction.

Academic Pressure

The pressure on kids to achieve and achieve some more is increasing every day. This pressure ends up being a hamster wheel from which kids just can't seem to get off. The increased drive of their peers results in a competitive environment in which the stakes keep getting higher.

Increased competition for spots at universities paired with a highly competitive job market and parents who struggle with the individual competitiveness discussed earlier, places pressure on young people like never before.

Can these higher expectations be good for some kids? Sure.

Can these higher expectations be disastrous for some kids? Sure.

It all depends on the individual's personality and the degree of exposure and vulnerability to mental health disorders.

Perfectionism, as noted earlier, is often assumed to be related to improved performance. Academic performance is no different. So for some students, yes, the pressure drives better performance and they don't experience significant negative side effects.

However, for these students, perfectionism does not necessarily make them better at what they are doing academically, which is learning. Rather, perfectionism causes them to want better grades and worry more about them. The constant positive reinforcement of excellent grades and results pushes students to raise the bar higher and higher.

When students begin seeing academic perfection as the standard rather than academic success, then we have a problem. Learning becomes not only a responsibility but a burden.

Academic success is, not surprisingly, thought to be a positive outcome whether it is related to perfectionism or not.

But this assumption requires a bit of reconsideration. Studies have shown that academic success comes with certain downsides. Young people can begin to strive for perfection that doesn't exist and therefore never achieve a feeling of satisfaction. They can develop fear of failure that can be crippling. Young people with perfectionistic tendencies can also end up losing respect for self and respect of others because of these tendencies.

How students see their academic selves is the critical element. How they interpret success and failure needs to be reestablished with young people. The concepts of growth mindset and fixed mindset are gaining traction within the educational community and aim to show young people that personal effort and improvement is the end goal—not some illusory pie-in-the-sky idea of perfection.

How students see all of these achievements fitting into the bigger picture is also important. With a nose to the grindstone approach to academics, some children can lose sight of why they are working so hard. What is the purpose? Where are they headed? Positive and negative perfectionism can play a significant role here.

Studies of high school freshmen have shown that academic pressure for those who lean more toward negative perfectionism creates fear of failure and depression. For these young people, parental pressure was perceived as a more serious problem.

What's more is negative perfectionism is not associated with improvements in academic achievement contrary to popular belief. So essentially the costs for these young people are quite high while the payoff is negligible.

For those young people who have more positive perfectionistic tendencies, academic pressure was correlated with motivation, hope of success and achievement. However, depression was still an issue.

At the end of the day, the way students react to academic pressure will depend on the student and their individual experience and coping mechanisms.

The difference between pressure turning a lump of coal into dust or a diamond is often negligible and that seems to also be the case here. Many different factors contribute to the uncontrollable circumstances in life and the way young people perceive those events, cope and react.

Combating Perfectionism in Young People

Brené Brown is a research professor at the University of Houston. She studies courage, vulnerability, shame and empathy. She likens perfection to the passing lane on a highway and cautions that it should only be used for passing.

She says, "What makes constant assessing and comparing so self-defeating is that we are often comparing our lives, our marriages, our families and our communities to unattainable media-driven visions of perfection." (Brown, 2012, p26).

In order to help young people thrive in today's environment, parents, teachers, and professionals must support them and inform them of the downsides of consistently trying to be perfect.

Fortunately, there are many things that can be done to help young people steer clear of perfectionism. Below are just a few strategies that have been tailored for the experiences of young people. The general strategies discussed in Chapter 7 can be applied as well.

Growth Mindset vs. Fixed Mindset

The first step in combating perfectionism is distinguishing between an achievement-oriented state and a progress-oriented state. Here we are essentially talking about enjoying the journey rather than simply focusing on the destination.

To do this, a discussion about mindset is necessary. Some aspects of societies, families, and schools often unintentionally promote a perfectionist mindset. In situations like these, young people learn that anything less than a perfect outcome is a failure.

They view the entire process as a waste of time. This mindset, however, can and should be changed in order to see and find value in the mistakes along the way as necessary steps in the growth process.

Learning how the brain operates and that it is possible to direct thought patterns and overall mindset is a powerful strategy in combating perfectionism.

A growth mindset says that ability can be developed. When young people operate with a growth mindset, they begin to understand that it is possible to develop over time.

Young people with a fixed mindset believe that their abilities are fixed and that the needle can only be moved with relentless hard work and determination.

Beliefs about their inherent ability and the potential for growth or change have a significant impact on how young people experience life and respond to setbacks and adversity.

Young people that operate with a fixed mindset tend to avoid challenges, give up easily when faced with struggling and fall into dangerous patterns of depression and anxiety because of false beliefs about their ability and potential.

However, those who operate using a growth mindset can begin to see setbacks as opportunities to grow and learn. They are also more likely to push themselves in difficult situations and move beyond perceived personal limitations.

Let's look at a few examples:

Example 1

The Fixed Mindset thinks:

Everyone else in class is meeting for study group tonight, but I am tired and am not going. Why am I so lazy?

The Growth Mindset thinks:

What I need tonight is food and rest. With a good night of rest and sleep, I can always join that group tomorrow. I'm not going to feel bad about it all night.

Example 2

The Fixed Mindset thinks:

I wasn't selected for the team. The coach must have thought I'm not very athletic.

The Growth Mindset thinks:

That coach doesn't know what I'm capable of. I'm going to practice over the coming year and try out again next year when I've developed the skills I saw in the players who are more advanced and experienced than I am. I know what to do.

Example 3

The Fixed Mindset thinks:

I don't have as many Instagram likes as my best friend. I just must not be as likeable and interesting as she is.

The Growth Mindset thinks:

I know that judging my worth based on Instagram likes is a problem and that I'm not alone in experiencing this problem. I know there are strategies I can learn to improve my self-esteem. I don't have to feel this way. I can grow and change.

When perfectionists become aware of the difference between these two mindsets, they begin to realize they have a choice.

Resilience

In school, perfectionists only raise their hand if they are absolutely certain they have the right answer. As that student learns about resilience, they begin to realize making mistakes is completely acceptable and actually encouraged in the learning process.

Resilience is particularly important when a perfectionist encounters a setback like a bad grade, a social rejection or a goal left unachieved.

Resilience isn't a skill that we are all born with. Some children, teens and even young adults don't know anything about resilience. This is a major problem, especially for perfectionists.

Resilience and the awareness of it can be developed in many ways.

Journaling and Gratitude

Through journal writing, young people can write about a setback, rather than just replaying it over and over in the mind. This can help make sense of what went wrong and what can be done differently next time. Young people can begin to realize that the setback isn't as bad as they initially thought. Taking time to acknowledge your inherent perseverance helps develop resilience.

When you journal about the future and the different steps you can take, you are helping yourself develop resilience. It's ok if you don't even know what the next steps are. Just opening yourself up to the possibilities will help prevent ruminating about the negative event.

By journaling, you can also open up your mind to the aforementioned concept of growth mindset.

Incorporate growth mindset when writing about resilience. See mistakes as growth opportunities rather than only as blunders.

Flexibility and gratitude also help develop resilience. Use your journal in different ways. One day, list items for which you're grateful. This helps to emphasize the positive and diminish the negatives. The next day, try something different.

Reframing

Young people should be encouraged to see mistakes as a natural part of life and a path to growth. Parents should redirect the thinking of their children, whether they struggle with perfectionism or not, to see criticism or setbacks not as signs that the child is lacking, but as a sign that the child is learning and growing instead. Or if a serious mistake was made, consider it as an opportunity to change strategy or adjust the level of effort in order to achieve better outcomes in the future.

Parental Modeling

As in other areas of parenting, modeling behavior that demonstrates self-acceptance and self-forgiveness is critically important. Recognize when you, the parent, are overestimating expectations for yourself and of course for your child as well.

Be willing to take risks and make mistakes in front of your children. Then do your best to handle the failure gracefully. Even if you fail in that regard, don't miss the opportunity to admit you were too harsh on yourself and that you realize everyone makes mistakes and being easy on yourself when you make one is not always easy, but it is wildly important to keep trying.

By recognizing the constant stream of messages about perfection that children are receiving, parents can and should address and challenge those messages together with their children. Those who take this difficult challenge will help their children become more resilient, healthier and happier individuals.

Points to Remember:

- In many families, perfectionism is encouraged, knowingly or unknowingly.
- Children don't have the cognitive ability to differentiate between normal expectations and abusive expectations.
- Children can also learn perfectionism just by growing up around highly successful parents, perfectionists or not, who model perfection through expectations for themselves and their behavior.
- Children can impose perfection on themselves.
- Society, the media, and especially social media have a significant influence on perfectionism.
- Social media also triggers the fear of missing out, commonly known as FOMO.
- The pressure on kids today to achieve and achieve some more is increasing every day.
- How students see their academic selves is the critical element. How they interpret success and failure needs to be reestablished with young people.
- The concepts of growth mindset and fixed mindset are gaining traction within the educational community and aim to show

young people that personal effort and improvement is the end goal - not some illusory pie-in-the-sky idea of perfection.
- In order to help young people thrive in today's environment, parents, teachers, and professionals must support them and inform them of the downsides of consistently trying to be perfect.
- When children learn about resilience, they begin to realize making mistakes is completely acceptable and actually encouraged in the learning process.
- Through journal writing, young people can write about a setback, rather than just replaying it over and over in the mind.
- Parents should redirect the thinking of their children, whether they struggle with perfectionism or not, to see criticism or setbacks not as signs that the child is lacking, but as a sign that the child is learning and growing instead.
- Parents can model behavior that demonstrates self-acceptance and self-forgiveness.

Chapter 6:
Perfectionism in Adults

Relatively few studies exist for perfectionism in adults. Experts hypothesize that the reason may be an incorrect notion that as we age, perfectionism tends to go away. But this is not the case.

Perfectionism in the Workplace

Health

Perfectionists are already at increased risk for stress and anxiety among other issues. It certainly doesn't help matter that the career paths often embarked upon by perfectionists in medicine, law, engineering and publishing require stringent standards. Not surprisingly, perfectionists find themselves at an elevated risk of becoming workaholics.

Characteristics associated with workaholics include exhaustion and chronic stress. When you are tired and lacking energy, you are vulnerable to illness.

Women

A recent study showed that women in the corporate workforce are much more likely to demonstrate perfectionistic characteristics than their male counterparts. Psychologist Peta Slocombe, senior vice president of corporate health at Medibio, the organization that conducted the study said, "If you're going to be perfectionistic about telling the kids you're going to be there when you're going to be there, that's one thing," she warned. "But if you're going to be perfectionistic about what you make the kids for lunch in the morning, as well as never missing an email at work, and every other thing, that's another" (Ward, 2018, para 13).

Some will point to the fact that girls were raised with different expectations than boys. Although the expectations may have been unintended or unconsciously held, they were gender based even in progressive-leaning families and schools. Girls are often rewarded for being obedient and diligent. Boys are expected to be adventurous and mischievous.

In the workplace, entry level positions lend themselves to obedient and diligent work, but as you climb the corporate ladder, the childhood qualities expected in boys lead to the qualities—like risk taking, creativity and boldness—that are rewarded in the corporate environment.

This is why women must let go of perfectionistic tendencies, take risks, and give themselves permission to make a mistake here and there. By doing this, you try new things, and become that much more innovative.

Taking risks and making mistakes leads to problem-solving skills, confidence and leading by example. Arguably, however, the most important aspect of making mistakes is demonstrating the fact that you are human. Not perfect, just human.

Not to mention the fact that no one ever said I love working for a perfectionist.

Results

It's often said that you shouldn't allow perfection to get in the way of good. There is a trade-off when a perfectionist works on your team. If they get the job done, great. It might be sensational. But there is a good chance the job does not get done. Heck, there is a chance the job does not even get started for reasons of procrastination we addressed earlier.

Business leaders realize this trade-off. Somewhere between perfect and good enough is where the magic happens. And somewhere in there lies the results that the most successful business leaders are seeking.

Consider this. You have a critical task that is do or die for your business. It could be the launch of a new product's marketing campaign or designing a demo for a new product feature on your site. You have two people on your team. You must hand off the task to one of these two.

Employee A is a capable person who has proven to be efficient and to consistently put forward a good effort. She does her best. If you hand the task off to Employee A, you can be sure she will get it done. It might not knock your socks off, but it will be good.

Employee B is a stereotypical perfectionist. She will promise to produce outstanding results. You know from experience that she has a tendency to overpromise and underdeliver. If she completes the project, it will be amazing but it will most certainly be late and might take even twice as long as you expect.

What would you do?
This is the irony inside the riddle of perfectionism.

Perfectionism at Home

Many can attest to trying to create a Martha Stewart version of themselves. Martha Stewart finds no shame in being a perfectionist. In fact, she once told Oprah Winfrey that being a perfectionist is why she is so successful.

However, many women without a team supporting their every move find it a daunting act to follow. Consider this advice from Stewart for organizing linens. Yes, you read that right, organizing linens:

> "There's something incredibly satisfying about opening up the linen closet to see not unholy chaos but color-coded bundles neatly tied in a bow. To keep bed linens organized, fold each set—pillowcases and both top and fitted sheets—and wrap with a 1 1/2-yard square of fabric inspired by Japanese furoshiki. Then, using like colors, coordinate the sets by room or by sheet size, and shelve them together. This method makes finding the linen set you need a snap.
>
> Bed linens shelved by type-fitted sheets stacked next to pillowcases quickly become disordered when you try to retrieve them to put together matching sets.

> Try this method instead: Slip each set into one of its pillowcases, and store the sets by size—twin, full, and so on—with colors, trim, or other defining details clearly visible."
> (Stewart, n.d., para 10-12)

I mean, who can keep up with that? Of course a nicely organized linen closet is a good thing this website is filled with guidance similar to this. Images of perfect linen closets, perfectly stocked pantries and refrigerators, and perfectly nutritious meals on the table each and every day, can take a toll over time.

Of course, Martha Stewart is not entirely to blame. Social media not only applies pressure to children to be perfectionists, but to adults as well.

Between the perfect linen closet from Martha Stewart to the perfect shiplap walls we see on HGTV to the images of perfect children in the Vineyard Vines catalog, images of perfection are everywhere. According to Ann Smith, an author who studies and writes about perfection:

If a perfectionist mother has a career or a job that is stressful and demanding, guilt becomes a constant companion. When my children were young and I was a single parent with a challenging job, I remember having a constant feeling that wherever I was, I felt like I should be somewhere else. I kept pushing through and tried to be the best in both areas without falling apart. When the kids went to bed, I would collapse, sometimes cry and start all over again the next day. (2013, para 12).

Perfectionism and Parenting

Perfectionists who are parents not only have issues at work and with their health, but also have an internal pressure to raise perfect kids. Perfectionist parents think they are expected to produce popular, accomplished, happy and successful children. They figure, if I can control my own life, I can control how my kids turn out.

However, 1+1 doesn't equal 2 when it comes to parenting.
Add to all of this stress the competition that parents experience among one another.

Competition among mothers is fierce and can trigger perfectionistic behavior. Often caught between wisdom of family and current environmental trends, the pressure on new mothers is incredible.

- Should I breastfeed or not?
- Is a pacifier really the end of the world?
- Am I engaging enough with my child?

Then just as you get the hang of it, your kids continue to grow. Adolescence is a trying time for parents and children. But perfectionistic parents have an especially hard time. Teens struggle with a variety of issues during adolescence. Perfectionist parents may focus so heavily on their child's academic and social status, that they unintentionally pile on additional pressure during this very tumultuous time. This can be a recipe for disaster.

Much more important for adolescent development are skills such as kindness, creativity and resilience.

Perfectionism and parenting is such a pervasive problem that it might just be a sequel to this book, but in short, research proves that it produces the opposite of the intended results:

Adolescents must make mistakes in order to learn and grow. This is especially important while they still live with their parents in what is hopefully a loving environment. When parents establish open and accepting relationships, teens will be more likely to share their struggles.

Perfectionistic parents convey the message that parents need the kids to be ok so the parents can be ok. That is a lot of pressure for a kid. Kids whose perfectionist parents try too hard can experience diminished self-esteem when they disappoint their parents.

Children learn from how parents act much more than from how parents tell the children to act so finding solutions to combat perfectionism are increasingly important for parents.

Perfectionism and Aging

Many believe that as we grow older and wiser, perfectionism will just ride off into the sunset. This is often not the case.

For adults who struggle with perfection, it is especially important that they address the problem since high expectations that were difficult to achieve when they were younger are likely to become increasingly out of reach as they get older and become unable to perform in the same capacity.

Perfectionism and Marriage

For the spouse of a perfectionist, life can be a challenge. Without meaning to, the perfectionist spouse is critical of everything the other spouse does. Although the perfectionist sees the criticism as helping the other spouse cook, clean, dress and even do their jobs the 'right' way, it is incredibly insulting to the other spouse and can cause a breakdown in the marriage.

The perfectionist spouse sees the behavior one way: They are helping the other spouse toward self-improvement.

The other spouse sees it very differently: They will never measure up or satisfy the expectations of the perfectionist spouse.

Nothing that spouse does seems to measure up. The standards of the perfectionist spouse are impossibly high and can cause irreparable harm to a marriage.
This is especially true for parents:
Couples tend to talk about what the children need, the everyday schedule and to-do list, the honey-dew list for items that require attention around the house, but they make little time to talk about anxiety and worry that perfectionists often experience.

This can damage the relationship as intimacy becomes compromised over time.

How Can you Prevent Perfectionism from Hurting your Marriage?

Look for Things Your Partner Does Right

Yes, it's very easy to see the mistakes and missteps your partner makes. It is easy to find problems within your marriage. You may have the best of intentions and think that identifying and finding problems is helping the marriage, but it isn't.

It is much harder to seek out and recognize all of the things that your partner does well. Look for the good things. Remember, what you focus on becomes bigger. Start the day by setting an intention to find three positive things your partner does or positive character traits they possess. Then communicate those things to them. Not only will this help train your mind to operate this way going forward, but it will strengthen the bond in your marriage.

Realize that Your Way Isn't the Only Way to Do Things

When your spouse does something for you in an effort to help, don't correct or criticize. Even if you are absolutely certain that the way they did that certain thing is incorrect, leave it alone.

Maybe you feel that the dishwasher needs to be loaded in a certain way. You are not necessarily right. And even when you are, your spouse may feel differently. It just may not be that important to them. It is important to recognize your spouse's opinion. Doing anything other than that is a losing battle. Your spouse feels disrespected when that happens.

Stop Sweating the Small Stuff

The next time you want to criticize something, ask yourself: Does it really matter? Is it worth it?
Putting things in perspective helps evaluate what really matters. Is the way your spouse makes the bed really a problem that needs to be addressed? Is it worth an argument and the negative feelings that will result?

Put on Your Own Oxygen Mask

This metaphor gets a lot of play, maybe too much. But it applies in this case. Self-compassion and self-care are essential for a healthy marriage. Emotionally healthy people understand the importance of treating themselves with grace and kindness. When you take care of your physical and emotional health, you can decrease the pressure you are putting on yourself.
When you feel better, you can then treat others with more compassion and care.

Have More Fun

This sounds like an odd directive. But for perfectionists, who often choose work over fun, it is critically important. Making time to relax both alone and with your partner will enable you to embrace opportunities for fun. This enables the two of you to build intimacy that will strengthen your marriage.

Admit Your Struggle with Perfectionism

Although it's likely your spouse has already figured this out, admitting your struggle with perfectionism can be an important first step in healing the marriage.

When you admit why certain things are so important to you, you help your spouse understand that you are struggling with something. By being vulnerable in this way, you are likely to deepen intimacy in your marriage.

Deep connections result when we share our personal challenges and fears. Maybe by talking you will even begin to further understand things about your past that have influenced your need for perfection.

Points to Remember:

- Just as for children, adults are receiving societal pressure to be perfect.
- Perfectionistic adults find themselves at an elevated risk of becoming workaholics.
- Women in the corporate workforce are much more likely to demonstrate perfectionistic characteristics than their male counterparts.
- Taking risks and making mistakes leads to problem-solving skills, confidence and leading by example.
- Somewhere between perfect and good enough is where the magic happens. And somewhere in there lies the results that the most successful business leaders are seeking.
- Perfectionist parents think they are expected to produce popular, accomplished, happy and successful children. They figure, if I can control my own life, I can control how my kids turn out.

- For the spouse of a perfectionist, life can be a challenge. Without meaning to, the perfectionist spouse is critical of everything the other spouse does.
- For older adults, high expectations that were difficult to achieve when they were younger are likely to become increasingly out of reach as they get older.

Chapter 7:
Strategies for Self-Acceptance

Managing perfectionist tendencies is a delicate balancing act. It requires using positive personality traits to achieve happiness and stability while working hard to counteract some of the destructive patterns of perfectionism that impact mental well-being. There are several actions perfectionists can focus on to perform more effectively

Making positive changes to deeply ingrained habits and behaviors is difficult, to say the least. It requires self-examination, self-acceptance and a general rewiring of thought patterns.

Gratitude

Perfectionists operate using the belief that who they are isn't really enough. No matter what you do, no matter how much you achieve, no matter how hard you try - you are always striving for this illusory destination that just does not exist.

Essentially, perfectionists operate from a place of emptiness and an idea of lack. You feel you are lacking. Your efforts are lacking. Your friends are lacking. It's a vicious cycle where nobody wins.

There is a theory that what you focus on becomes bigger. This is true for perfectionists.

You focus on everything you don't have, so that is all you see.

Gratitude turns that inside out. It takes a sledgehammer to that way of thinking and turns on a light in a dark room.

Gratitude repositions your mind's camera from the subject of not enough to the subject of enough.
Think about that camera for a moment.

You are at a party and you are the photographer. There is one couple who is fighting and you follow them all night photographing them. Think about the photos you'd have at the end of the party.

There is another couple who is having a good time. Not even a great time - just a good time. They smile here and there. They talk to others. You might even be able to snap a few shots of them holding hands.
What do those pictures look like at the end of the night?

If you showed both sets of pictures to someone who had not been at the party, they would see two very different events even though the pictures were taken at the same place.

It's the same with perfectionism and gratitude. What you focus on becomes bigger.

Focus on the lack. Experience more lack.
Focus on the abundance. Experience more abundance.

Practical Ways to Practice Gratitude

Sure. Focus on the positive. Sounds great, but how do I do that? There are many ways to begin practicing gratitude. Below are only a few.

Gratitude journal. Start by grabbing a journal or a notebook that you'll dedicate only to gratitude. You are trying to change the way your brain is wired here, so it's not going to happen overnight. It takes small steps, but they must be consistent.

The only rule is that you should write every day. Some people list three things that happened during the day—big or small—that they are grateful for.

Some like to have a list of sentence starters, so there is one below. It can be one sentence, a paragraph, bullets, whatever you want. Just write.

If you are not a pen and paper person, there are many apps out there also. Give some thought to which option would be better before simply jumping at the tech option. You know how distracting your phone can be. To really dedicate yourself to this practice, pen and paper is best for allowing you the time and focus you'll need to reflect.

Focus on being grateful for who you are. We'll get to gratitude about your place in life, your accomplishments and all of those types of things. Underneath all of that is a dark belief that you are not enough, so start there.

- Repeat a simple mantra as you meditate, walk or exercise - *I am enough.*
- Create a list of things you like about yourself; character and personality traits, kind things you've done, talents, even things about your physical appearance are important to appreciate. Look at the list at the beginning of each day to remind yourself to maintain a gratitude focus throughout the day.
- Use your journal to complete this sentence once in a while, or every day: *I am grateful because I am...*

Dinner table. Some families practice gratitude to get the conversation going at the dinner table or at any meal. Going around the table and saying one thing you are thankful for is a great way to learn about each other's days and ingrain a positive lifelong habit.

There are several variations for this strategy. One way to summarize your day that incorporates gratitude and life's challenges is called Rose-Bud-Thorn. Each person shares one of each.

Rose: The rose is the gratitude portion. What were you thankful for? It could be the sun on your face during a morning walk. It could be the kind gesture someone at the table performed as you sat down to eat.

Bud: The bud is something you are looking forward to in the coming days. Perhaps it's as simple as a good night sleep or a relaxing weekend.

Thorn: The thorn provides an opportunity for kids and adults to share something that was difficult from their day or an upcoming event they are feeling down about. Not only does talking about something like this often help put it in perspective, but it allows everyone at the table to understand that person a bit better.

Gratitude 'beads'. This strategy borrows the concept from rosary beads although the gratitude beads do not necessarily need to be beads. A necklace, bracelet or watch will suffice. You could even use buttons on your shirt. Choose a time of day—maybe on your commute home—where touch each one of the 'beads' and focus on something for which you feel gratitude.

Be patient. Gratitude doesn't come easy to everyone. For some it is easier said than done. If you aren't feeling grateful for anything, allow yourself to feel that way for a moment. Parents often tell their teenagers who want something they don't have to be grateful for the plate of food in front of them or the roof over their head, but that doesn't work.

Gratitude must come from within. So if you are struggling to feel grateful, be patient with yourself. Begin with the smallest of things. Take a deep breath. Your lungs are working. That is something you can be grateful for. Go for a walk. Your legs are working. Again, something to be grateful for. From there it will get easier and become more natural.

Vulnerability

According to Brené Brown, embracing vulnerability is a key component in understanding and overcoming perfectionism. She says, "there's a significant difference between perfectionism and healthy striving or striving for excellence. Perfectionism is the belief that if we do things perfectly and look perfect, we can minimize or avoid the pain of blame, judgment, and shame. Perfectionism is a twenty-ton shield that we lug around, thinking it will protect us, when in fact it's the thing that's really preventing us from being seen" (Schawbel, 2013, para 17).

Brown says that perfectionism is also very different from self-improvement. Perfectionism, at its core, is about trying to earn approval. Brown believes that most perfectionists grew up being praised for achievement and performance about grades, manners, rule following, people pleasing, appearance and sports. Then somewhere along the way, they adopted a debilitating belief system that tells them:
I am my accomplishments. How well I accomplish things tells everyone what kind of person I am.
And leaves kids asking the question: *What will everyone think?*

Perfectionism is other-focused, so kids naturally become stuck in a cycle of please, perform, perfect, repeat.

Healthy striving, on the other hand, is self-focused. Children should be asking:
How can I improve?
Brown has learned that "perfectionism is not a way to avoid shame. Perfectionism is a form of shame. Where we struggle with perfectionism, we struggle with shame." (Schawbel, 2013, para 20)

Vulnerability and authenticity require practice. When you walk into a room, will you let yourself be seen? That is a choice. To make a choice like this you need to let go of the idea of faking it.

Sometimes, you are surrounding yourself with wrong people and it will be impossible to be authentic and vulnerable. They're faking it, so you find you need to fake it. We all have times when we pretend to be something that we are not. Once you identify that problem, you can solve it.

Perfectionists are at risk for a multitude of missed opportunities. Perfectionism steals the joy from life. Many believe that there is an antidote and that antidote is vulnerability. Brown believes that vulnerability is having the courage to show up when you know there is no controlling the outcome. Here's how you can adopt vulnerability in your journey to overcoming perfection:

1. Accept the Messiness in Life

Perfectionists are often accused of being procrastinators because they don't want to do anything that won't turn out perfect. The fact is this: Nothing is perfect and the timing is never right.

Perfectionists also think to themselves, if I look perfect, work perfect, dress perfect and do just about every single thing perfect, then I can minimize or avoid pain and judgment. They are essentially always trying to outrun judgment, afraid that the world is going to see them as they really are and that they will just not measure up.

How much time have you wasted waiting for things to become perfect before taking a step forward toward a goal? How many opportunities have you squandered because you couldn't control every moving part in a situation?

Perfect doesn't exist and the sooner you accept the messiness in life and take action despite the mess, the sooner you begin really living your life.

2. Expect to Fail

Expect to fail. Hell, hope to fail. Not only is it a part of life, but it's proof that we're living. It's also the way that humans learn and improve.

Perfectionists are terrified of failure. They care what others think and they want those thoughts to be polished and perfect. Well, that is just not going to happen whether you continue on trying to make everything perfect or if you accept life as it is.

When you begin to embrace vulnerability, you begin to release that fear of failure and see it as part of the process. You are going to fail. Say it with me. You. Are. Going. To. Fail. And so am I. And so is the next person. And the next. You get the idea.

3. Link Vulnerability to Humility

The word vulnerability can sometimes get a bad rap. It has the connotation that an attack is imminent and we are ripe for the taking. Many see vulnerability as the opposite of courage, but in fact it is courage.

If we think of vulnerability the way we think of humility, perhaps it will be easier to adopt it as a new way of thinking.

Humility is being open, curious and collaborative. Humble people listen to others, ask meaningful questions and are interested in learning new things.
Too often perfectionists are too proud to seek help even when it is desperately needed. Pride can be destructive and is the opposite of humility. Pride might look like strength from a distance, but up close it reeks of stress and insecurity.

4. Visualize the Phoenix from the Flame

The idea of becoming vulnerable or of humbling yourself might terrify you. If so, you are not alone. However, in order to become more resilient and less tethered to perfection, you must first allow yourself to take off the armor and be vulnerable. Let it all hang out. When you show others you are not perfect, they will feel free to show you their real selves too. You free them to live honestly and you free yourself.

Imagine the phoenix emerging from the flame. You shed your armor, you burn your pride and you leave it there in the flames. When you emerge, there is no more perfection to cling to. Your flaws, when you have set them free, no longer have power over you. You will have naturally built up some resilience, authenticity and humanity.

5. Trust in Yourself and Others

To put yourself out there, warts and all, you need to know that you can handle it. You need to trust in the goodness of others. Trust that once they know the real you, the goodness in them will show you that they accept you even if you are not perfect. Maybe in the end they will accept you even more because you are not perfect.

And even if others are dealing with their own insecurities and do not react the way you had hoped, trust in yourself. Trust that you have the emotional strength to persevere through anything. Trust that you can do the hard work to embrace vulnerability and failure. Trust that you can learn the lessons necessary to overcome anything. Trust that you can fail and not hate yourself for it. Because it is possible.

Setting SMART Goals

Cognitive behavioral therapy, or CBT, is one type of treatment to combat perfectionism. With CBT, a behavior specialist challenges rigid thinking and unrealistic beliefs and encourages flexible thought processes and strategies for adopting and practicing self-acceptance. During CBT, specialists help those who struggle with perfectionism to set SMART goals—intentions that are Specific, Measurable, Attainable, Relevant and Time-bound.

Perhaps the most important letter in the acronym is A. Setting *attainable* goals is so vital to a perfectionist's mental well-being. The assessment of your individual opportunities and capabilities must be realistic, with sensible deadlines and reasonable goals. If you need to make the goal smaller, do so. If you need to extend the timeline, do it.

Meditation

Mindfulness, typically via meditation, is also becoming increasingly common, but does it work?
Experts think it does since perfectionists are not typically mindful by nature. Being mindful means staying present in the here and now. Perfectionists are usually obsessing about events in the past or in the future and have difficulty with mindfulness.

According to one study, musicians who mediated weekly reduced their anxiety about performing. The type of meditation did not seem to make a difference.
Another study looked at a variety of meditation techniques and how they impact a perfectionist's heart rate. The heart rate typically increases when feelings of anxiety are present and decrease with feelings of relaxation.

Subjects with perfectionistic tendencies were assigned a challenging task and were later told they had failed. Participants were randomly assigned to four groups:

- one rested without meditation

- one practiced muscle relaxation

- one practiced breathing-guided meditation

- one listened to a meditation urging them to stop judging themselves

All groups demonstrated a reduction in heart rate, but the heart of subjects in the last group who were urged to stop judging themselves through a guided meditation, had higher recovery rates than all other groups.

Researchers concluded that, although more research is necessary, mindfulness that focuses on removing judgment may be particularly important for perfectionists (Diaz, 2018).

The Importance of Breathing

- Breathing is something we do involuntarily. When perfectionists concentrate on slower, more effective breathing, they can experience significant results. Many don't give it much thought but it can provide many benefits including:
- Reducing anxiety and depression. The body is constantly trying to reach a place of balance and equilibrium. Because perfectionists experience higher levels of anxiety, the body is constantly working against that equilibrium. Breathing can calm the central nervous system which can help with both of these issues.

- Fostering a sense of calm. When you intentionally slow your breathing, your heart beat stabilizes and your mind is able to focus. This helps to minimize the tendency many perfectionists have to ruminate or catastrophize.

A Few Techniques

There are many breathing techniques that can help perfectionists. Here are just a few.

Count to Ten. Focus energy on your breath and count out ten breaths. Sounds simple, but the chances that you will become distracted are pretty good. If you get distracted, forgive yourself and try again.

Forward Bend. First, stand tall and take a deep breath. Place the palms of your hands on your lower back. Take another deep breath. Next, slowly bend forward from your waist. Keep breathing slowly and bend as far as you can while still being comfortable.

Head, Shoulders, Knees and Toes. Try this breathing technique when you have trouble falling asleep.

First, simply focus on your breathing. Then move your attention to the top of your head. Dedicate one breath in and out to relaxing your head. Next move the focus to your eyes. Take another breath and release any tension that may exist. Continue down your body, breath by breath.

The goal here is to notice your breathing habits. Shallow breathing is less relaxing. So focus on deep breathing and whatever technique works the best for you.

Redefining Success and "Failure"

Success

What is your personal definition of success?
If you immediately thought of another person - whether that person is someone to whom you compare yourself or whether that person is someone you feel is judging you - you have identified a critical area for improvement. Too often, perfectionists employ comparative thinking.

This type of thinking needs to stop and your idea of success requires immediate redefining. Subconscious patterns can easily turn into habits over time and become internalized.

Consider this phrase: *This is the best next step in my career.*

Of course, career can be replaced with academic career, personal life, athletic achievement, etc.
Consider adjusting it to redefine success and let go of perfect. Maybe it would look like this:
*This is the best next step in my career **for me at this point in my life**.*

When a perfectionist makes this adjustment, it takes the expectation from a general ideal that keeps you striving for bigger and better to something that is personalized for you and the particular point in your journey.

Failure

First, rid yourself of the all-or-nothing mindset.
In any aspect of life, there is no achievement with failure. Athletes don't win championships without setbacks during the course of their preparation.

Corporate moguls didn't ride a smooth wave all the way to the board room. The most successful of inventors bombed over and over again until they figured out how to solve a problem.

Everything happens in a trial and error way, as a process. Nothing goes from start to finish perfectly.

Tech companies in Silicon Valley like Google, Apple and Facebook all have had their share of struggles. And guess what? They all encourage failure.

There is actually a saying in Silicon Valley: Fail fast and fail often.

Scroll through TedTalks and you can find hundreds of successful people laying it all out there. Their failures, embarrassing moments, you name it.

There is even an annual conference in over a dozen cities around the world that celebrates failure: FailCon. FailCon, just like ComicCon or any other convention, encourages startup founders to learn from and prepare for failure, so they can create their next iteration and keep on growing.

All of these leaders recognize that failure is essential to success. In fact, it paves the way for success to happen. So go on, fail quickly. Get it over with and then do it again. And again.

Second, realize that contextualizing disappointment is the next critical step in redefining failure.
Putting disappointments in perspective can help lessen the blow. When a plan doesn't materialize perfectly, take a step back.

Where you made mistakes, acknowledge them, take responsibility and move on.

However, consider other factors that may have been out of your control. Unpack the event and spot areas where the goal was either unrealistic or unpredictable.

Then seek to identify the silver linings within the "failure."

If you didn't get a promotion, consider that maybe you were meant to remain in your current role. Maybe something better is ahead and if you had gotten that promotion, things wouldn't have worked out as we planned. In other words, maybe that failure wasn't a failure at all, but just another step on your journey.

Remember the saying: *We make plans and God laughs.*

Points to Remember:

In preparing this chapter, I read through myriads of websites and scholarly online journals and rifled through the aisles of the bookstores to bring you solutions that will help in your search for a solution.

However, when perfectionist tendencies refuse to be eradicated and continue to be a persistent problem, it may be time to consider seeking the help of a mental health professional who can offer expert advice. There are solutions out there. Don't give up.

- When you develop awareness around their thinking, you can identify triggers and begin the work to end perfectionistic habits.
- When journals are used as a tool of reference, you can begin to identify and celebrate your achievements and reflect upon how that hard work has paid dividends.
- You can identify strategies that work and those that do not.
- The more you know yourself, the more you can control yourself, your thought patterns and your perfectionistic tendencies.

- When you become aware of negative thoughts, you can keep them at bay and cultivate habits that encourage positive thoughts to replace them.
- Resilience is a key component in combating perfectionism. Adjusting your reaction to setbacks and adversity is the first step in self-acceptance.
- What you focus on becomes bigger.
- Gratitude repositions your mind's camera from the subject of not enough to the subject of enough.
- Embracing vulnerability is a key component in understanding and overcoming perfectionism.
- Setting attainable goals is so vital to a perfectionist's mental well-being.
- Being mindful means staying present in the here and now.
- Mindfulness that focuses on removing judgment may be particularly important for perfectionists.
- The benefits that proper breathing can provide are staggering and should not be overlooked.
- Redefine your definition of success and failure.

Chapter 8:
Mini-Lessons

So in the end, how can we harness the positives of perfectionism while protecting ourselves from the negative implications? It is unrealistic to think we can rid ourselves of ingrained habits overnight or without help from others. It is not unrealistic to think that we can take steps in the right direction each and every day. And when we make mistakes and revert back into perfectionistic habits, we can brush ourselves off and try again.

To keep perfection in check, this chapter will provide some quick mini-lessons to refresh your commitment to the cause.

Mini-Lessons

Mini-Lesson #1:
See the Big Picture

Being a perfectionist isn't easy is it? In fact, it's downright exhausting.

But since it's in your nature, when you try to eradicate yourself of it, you're not going to suddenly go from shooting for the stars to shooting for the third floor. No way. No one should shoot for the third floor. What you should do, however, is focus some attention on the big picture. Ask yourself some tough questions:

- How much time do I spend on perfection? Is it getting out of control?
- Is it productive?
- What else could I be doing with that time?
- Am I spending time unnecessarily?
- At what point can I call the effort good enough?

Decide to be less perfect about a few things so that in the end, the big picture is as good as it can be without allowing you to revert to old habits. Focus on maximizing the time you do spend and remind yourself that you always give it your best effort, so the amount of time you spend should be enough.

Mini-Lesson #2:
Recalibrate Your Standards

Unless you are writing an inauguration speech for POTUS, your work and the time and effort to be spent on it could probably use some perspective. Again, questioning yourself is effective:

- At what point is this work good enough to show to someone for an informal opinion?
- How will I learn from the feedback of another person?

Maybe the work is good enough when you feel you are only a quarter of the way through. Imagine how much time you could save and what you could do with that time!

Mini-Lesson #3:
Set a Budget

We use budgets to keep our monetary spending in check. What if budgeting our time could keep perfectionism in check? Well, it can! And it should.

Perfectionists are on a journey to nowhere since perfection is an illusion. If we put roadblocks up at periodic points, in the form of a budgeted checklist along the journey to reroute the journey to a finite destination, perfectionism becomes restricted.

Take a report for school, for example. The perfectionist might stress over the topic choice and never get started. If we set a timeline for selection of topic by 6 pm on Saturday, the perfectionist is much more likely to get it done. The perfectionist now has a process with distinct goals that can be measured and ticked off the list.

Mini-Lesson #4:
Interrupt the Pattern

Perfectionists have a tendency to obsess, going over a thought or an activity or some work product with no end in sight and no productive reason for doing so. They feel obligated to think things through and feel as though doing so will produce some sort of solution. This, of course, is not true.

For those people who can remember what a record or a CD is, you'll remember that if it had a scratch it wouldn't keep spinning, so it wouldn't keep playing. The scratch caused an interruption. That is exactly what you need to do in your mind. Create an interruption of your thought pattern.

To do this:

Identify what triggers this behavior. Write down the patterns that you notice. Ask yourself, how can I avoid those triggers or deal with them when they arise?

Get some perspective. If you find yourself dwelling on a situation, you are likely focusing on the same things over and over again. Try to think about the situation differently. Either from someone else's point of view or in relation to much worse scenarios. Ask yourself, is this as big or as bad as I'm making it? Is spending time on this worth it?

Find a distraction. When you find yourself falling back into negative patterns, seek out work or something you enjoy to keep your mind occupied. Even taking a break for just a few minutes to get outside can lend perspective and break unwanted thought patterns.

Mini-Lesson #5:
Ask for Help

Share your perfectionism with someone. Whether it's a friend, a family member or a co-worker, be honest and let them know what has been going on.

Tell them you need someone to hold you accountable for making progress toward self-acceptance.

Give them permission to hold you accountable. Tell them you want them to let you know if they notice you being too hard on yourself or reaching for impossible standards.

Mini-Lesson #6:
Journal About Your Progress

At whatever interval you feel is right for you, reflect on the actions you are taking to work toward self-acceptance and move away from perfectionism.
Again, go to those difficult questions:

- What steps have I taken to be kinder to and more forgiving of myself?
- Were there any times I took a few steps backwards? How did I treat myself when this happened?
- Is there anything I'm avoiding for fear of making mistakes?
- Did I waste time trying to be perfect? Was it worth it?
- Were there times where I took a risk and did something when I knew it might not be perfect? Did I celebrate this progress?

As you journal, remember the journaling itself is an opportunity for you to demonstrate self-acceptance and self-forgiveness.

Conclusion

Perfectionists are their own toughest critics. Negative self-talk and self-neglect inevitably take their toll over time. You allow this to happen because you have not prioritized yourself in your planning.

It's almost as if you've plotted a map on the way to this perfect existence but forgot to account for the well-being of the driver.

You've forgotten to schedule breaks for eating and rest.

Well, it's time to take care of the driver.
Only when we begin respecting ourselves and our own personal need for self-care and self-love, can we really be on the right road and on the right journey.
I hope you will be able to use this book as a reference for many years to come as perfection is a struggle that doesn't go away.

Hopefully you can walk away loving yourself a little more by using this quick reference guide to remembering the most important ideas:

Stop negative self-talk and self-blame. The next time you find your negative voice piping up, recognize it and use the tools from this book to flip the switch and turn on your positive strategies.

When you make a mistake, instead of "how could I do that?" try "how can I fix this?"

When someone doesn't act the way you expected, instead of racking your brain to think of what you did to offend them, remind yourself that it likely has nothing to do with you.

In your everyday thought patterns, remember to incorporate phrases like:

- I'm a good person.
- I am doing my best.
- I'm working hard.
- I am always getting better.
- I love myself.

Focus on the positive. Remember what you focus on becomes bigger. What are two things you have done right today? What about yesterday? Focus on those things and visualize them over and over again. Let the good feelings wash over you and hold onto them.

Take care of yourself. Prioritize your physical and mental well-being. No one else is going to stop you from enforcing unrealistic expectations on yourself. You must commit to taking care of you. Ask yourself if you really want to be so hard on yourself for the next twenty years. Your future self will thank you. Attention to self-care has a cumulative effect over time. Consistent self-care can make a big difference later in life. Don't wait another minute.

References

Advisory Board. (2012, November 1). *Nature or nurture? Why some people are perfectionists.* Advisory Board.
https://www.advisory.com/daily-briefing/2012/11/01/why-some-people-are-perfectionists

Benson, Etienne. (2003, November). *The many faces of perfectionism.* American Psychological Association.
https://www.apa.org/monitor/nov03/manyfaces

Brown, B. (2012). Daring greatly: how the courage to be vulnerable transforms the way we live, love, parent, and lead. New York, NY: Penguin Random House.

Curran, T. (2019). *Perfectionism Is Increasing Over Time: A Meta-Analysis of Birth Cohort Differences From 1989 to 2016.* American Psychological Association.
https://www.apa.org/pubs/journals/releases/bul-bul0000138.pdf

Davis-Laack, P. (n.d.). *5 Styles of Perfectionism.* Stress & Resilience Institute.
https://stressandresilience.com/5-styles-of-perfectionism

Diaz, F. *Relationships Among Meditation, Perfectionism, Mindfulness, and Performance Anxiety Among Collegiate Music Students.* Sage Journals.
https://journals.sagepub.com/doi/abs/10.1177/0022429418765447

Fey, T. (2011, March 7). *Lessons from Late Night.* The New Yorker.
https://www.newyorker.com/magazine/2011/03/14/lessons-from-late-night

Flatow, I. (2011, November 11). *'Steve Jobs': Profiling An Ingenious Perfectionist.* NPR.
https://www.npr.org/2011/11/11/142244048/steve-jobs-profiling-an-ingenious-perfectionist

Flett, G. (2012, February 29.) *The Price of Perfectionism.* Association for Psychological Science.
https://www.psychologicalscience.org/observer/the-price-of-perfectionism

Haden, J. (n.d.). *Steve Jobs, and Why Perfection Might Be Your Worst Enemy.* Inc.com.
https://www.inc.com/jeff-haden/chasing-steve-jobs-why-perfectionism-is-your-worst-enemy.html

Hellman, E. (2016). *Keeping Up Appearances: Perfectionism and Perfectionistic Self-Presentation on Social Media.* DePauw University.
https://scholarship.depauw.edu/cgi/viewcontent.cgi?article=1048&context=studentresearch

Ibrahim, A. (2013, March). *A systematic review of studies of depression prevalence in university students.* Science Direct.
https://www.sciencedirect.com/science/article/abs/pii/S0022395612003573?via%3Dihub

Jarrett, C. (2017, July 27). *Perfectionism as a risk factor for suicide – the most comprehensive test to date.* The British Psychological Society. https://digest.bps.org.uk/2017/07/27/perfectionism-as-a-risk-factor-for-suicide-the-most-comprehensive-test-to-date

Kalpidou, M. (2011). *The relationship between Facebook and the well-being of undergraduate college students.* Pub Med.
https://pubmed.ncbi.nlm.nih.gov/21192765

Kaundinya, A. (2018, August 10). *5 Ways to Manage Your Type-A Personality.* The Cut. https://www.thecut.com/article/ways-to-manage-type-a-personality.html

Koerten, H. (2019, November 30). *Cardiovascular effects of brief mindfulness meditation among perfectionists experiencing failure.* Wiley Online Library.
https://onlinelibrary.wiley.com/doi/epdf/10.1111/psyp.13517

Lewis, P. (2017, Oct 6). *'Our minds can be hijacked': the tech insiders who fear a smartphone dystopia.* The Guardian.
https://www.theguardian.com/technology/2017/oct/05/smartphone-addiction-silicon-valley-dystopia

Rettner, R. (2010, July 11). *The Dark Side of Perfectionism Revealed.* Live Science. https://www.livescience.com/6724-dark-side-perfectionism-revealed.html

Robinson, R. (2019, May 30). *How Steve Jobs Learned to Embrace Failure and Saved Apple*. The Balance Small Business.
https://www.thebalancesmb.com/steve-jobs-and-how-embracing-failure-saved-apple-1200640

Schawbel, D. (2013, April 21). *Brene Brown: How Vulnerability Can Make Our Lives Better.* Forbes.
https://www.forbes.com/sites/danschawbel/2013/04/21/brene-brown-how-vulnerability-can-make-our-lives-better/#28f3561a36c7

Smith, A. (2013, May 9). *The Perils of Perfectionism in Motherhood.* Psychology Today.
https://www.psychologytoday.com/us/blog/healthy-connections/201305/the-perils-perfectionism-in-motherhood

Stewart, M. (n.d.). *How to Fold a Fitted Sheet—and Keep an Organized Linen Closet.* Martha Stewart.
https://www.marthastewart.com/269141/how-to-fold-a-fitted-sheet

Stoeber, J. (2013, September). *Perfectionism and social desirability: Students report increased perfectionism to create a positive impression.* Science Direct.
https://www.sciencedirect.com/science/article/abs/pii/S0191886913001967

Ward, M. (2018, April 17). *Women more likely to be perfectionists, anxious at work.* The Sydney Morning Herald.
https://www.smh.com.au/lifestyle/health-and-wellness/women-more-likely-to-be-perfectionistic-anxious-at-work-20180412-p4z971.html

Printed in Great Britain
by Amazon